D0758155

DISCARDED
Richmond Public Library

RACE, INCARCERATION, AND AMERICAN VALUES

31143007777056
365.6089 Loury
Loury, Glenn C.
Race, incarceration, and
American values

RACE, INCARCERATION, AND AMERICAN VALUES

Glenn C. Loury

Based on the 2007 Tanner Lectures on
Human Values at Stanford

A Boston Review Book

THE MIT PRESS Cambridge, Mass. London, England

Copyright © 2008 Massachusetts Institute of Technology

All rights reserved. No part of this book may be reproduced in any form by any electronic or mechanical means (including photocopying, recording, or information storage and retrieval) without permission in writing from the publisher.

MIT Press books may be purchased at special quantity discounts for business or sales promotional use. For information, please e-mail special_sales@mitpress.mit.edu or write to Special Sales Department, The MIT Press, 55 Hayward Street, Cambridge, MA 02142.

This book was set in Adobe Garamond by *Boston Review* and was printed and bound in the United States of America.

Loury, Glenn C.
  Race, incarceration, and American values / Glenn C. Loury ; with Pamela Karlan, Loïc Wacquant, and Tommie Shelby.
      p. cm.
  "A Boston Review book."
  ISBN 978-0-262-12311-2 (hardcover : alk. paper)
  1. Prisons and race relations—United States. 2. Prisoners—United States. 3. Race discrimination—United States. 4. Imprisonment—United States. 5. Criminal justice, Administration of—United States. 6. Justice, Administration of—United States. 7. Crime and race—United States. 8. United States—Race relations. I. Title.
  HV6197.U5L68 2008
  365'.608996073—dc22

                                           2008022921

10 9 8 7 6 5 4 3 2 1

For my grandchildren

CONTENTS

I

*Race, Incarceration,
and American Values*

THE EARLY 1990S WERE THE AGE OF drive-by shootings, drug deals gone bad, crack cocaine, and gangsta rap. Between 1960 and 1990, the annual number of murders in New Haven rose from 6 to 31, the number of rapes from 4 to 168, the number of robberies from 16 to 1,784—all this while the city's population declined by 14 percent. Crime was concentrated in central cities: in 1990, two-fifths of Pennsylvania's violent crimes were committed in Philadelphia, home to one-seventh of the state's population. The subject of crime dominated American domestic-policy debates.

Most observers at the time expected things to get worse. Consulting demographic tables and extrapolating trends, scholars and pundits warned the public to prepare for an onslaught, and for a new kind of criminal—the anomic, vicious, irreligious, amoral, juvenile "super predator." In 1996, one academic commentator predicted a "bloodbath" of juvenile homicides in 2005.

And so we prepared. Stoked by fear and political opportunism, but also by the need to address a very real social problem, we threw lots of people in jail, and when the old prisons were filled we built new ones.

But the onslaught never came. Crime rates peaked in 1992 and have dropped sharply since. Even as crime rates fell, however, imprisonment rates remained high and continued their upward march. The result, the current American prison system, is a leviathan unmatched in human history.

According to a 2005 report of the International Centre for Prison Studies in London, the United States—with 5 percent of the world's population—houses 25 percent of the world's inmates. Our incarceration rate (714 per 100,000 residents) is almost 40 percent greater than those of our nearest competitors (the Bahamas, Belarus, and Russia). Other industrial democracies, even those with significant crime problems of their own, are much less punitive: our incarceration rate is 6.2 times that of Canada, 7.8 times that of France, and 12.3 times that of Japan. We have a corrections sector that employs more Americans than the combined work forces of General Motors, Ford, and Wal-Mart, the three largest corporate employers in the country, and we are spending some $200 billion annually on law enforcement and corrections at all levels of government, a fourfold increase (in constant dollars) over the past quarter century.

Never before has a supposedly free country denied basic liberty to so many of its citizens. In December 2006, some 2.25 million persons were being held in the nearly 5,000 prisons and jails that are scattered across America's urban and rural landscapes. One-third of inmates in state prisons are violent criminals, convicted of homicide, rape, or robbery. But the other two-thirds consist mainly of property and drug offenders. Inmates are disproportionately drawn from the most disadvantaged parts of society. On average, state inmates have fewer than eleven years of schooling. They are also vastly disproportionately black and brown.

How did it come to this? One argument is that the massive increase in incarceration reflects the success of a rational public policy: faced with a compelling social problem, we responded by imprisoning people and succeeded in lowering crime rates. This argument is not entirely misguided. Increased incarceration does appear to have reduced crime somewhat. But by how much? Estimates of the share of the 1990s reduction in violent crime that can be attributed to the prison boom range from 5 percent to 25 percent. Whatever the number, analysts of all political stripes now agree that we long ago entered the zone of diminishing returns. The conservative scholar John Dilulio, who coined the term "super predator" in the early 1990s, was by the end of that decade declaring in *The Wall Street Journal*, "Two Million Prisoners Are Enough." But there was no political movement for getting America out of the mass-incarceration business. The throttle was stuck.

A more convincing argument is that imprisonment rates have continued to rise while crime rates have fallen because we have become progressively more punitive: not because crime has continued to explode (it hasn't), not because we made a smart policy choice, but because we have made a collective decision to increase the rate of punishment.

One simple measure of punitiveness is the likelihood that a person who is arrested will be subsequently incarcerated. Between 1980 and

2001, there was no real change in the chances of being arrested in response to a complaint: the rate was just under 50 percent. But the likelihood that an arrest would result in imprisonment more than doubled, from 13 to 28 percent. And because the amount of time served and the rate of prison admission both increased, the incarceration rate for violent crime almost tripled, despite the decline in the level of violence. The incarceration rate for nonviolent and drug offenses increased at an even faster pace: between 1980 and 1997 the number of people incarcerated for nonviolent offenses tripled, and the number of people incarcerated for drug offenses increased by a factor of eleven. Indeed, the criminal-justice researcher Alfred Blumstein has argued that none of the growth in incarceration between 1980 and 1996 can be attributed to more crime.

The growth was entirely attributable to a growth in punitiveness, about equally to growth in prison commitments per arrest (an indication of tougher prosecution or judicial sentencing) and to longer time served (an indication of longer sentences, elimination of parole or later parole release, or greater readiness to recommit parolees to prison for either technical violations or new crimes).

This growth in punitiveness was accompanied by a shift in thinking about the basic purpose of criminal justice. In the 1970s, the sociologist David Garland argues, the corrections system was commonly seen as a way to prepare offenders to rejoin society. Since then, the focus has shifted from rehabilitation to punishment and stayed there. Felons are no longer persons to be supported, but risks to be dealt with. And the way to deal with the risks is to keep them locked up. As of 2000, thirty-three states had abolished limited parole (up from seventeen in 1980), twenty-four states had introduced three-strikes laws (up from zero), and forty states had introduced truth-in-sentencing laws (up from three). The vast majority of these changes occurred in the 1990s, as crime rates fell.

This new system of punitive ideas is aided by a new relationship between the media, the politicians, and the public. A handful of cases—in which a predator does an awful thing to an innocent—get excessive media attention and engender public outrage. This attention typically bears no relation to the frequency of the particular type of crime, yet laws—such as three-strikes laws that give mandatory life sentences to nonviolent drug offenders—and political careers are made on the basis of the public's reaction to the media coverage of such crimes.

Despite a sharp national decline in crime, American criminal justice has become crueler and less caring than it has been at any other time in our modern history. Why?

The question has no simple answer, but the racial composition of prisons is a good place to start. The punitive turn in the nation's social policy—intimately connected with public rhetoric about responsibility, dependency, social hygiene, and the reclamation of public order—can be fully grasped only when viewed against the backdrop of America's often ugly and violent racial history: there is a reason why our inclination toward forgiveness and the extension of a second chance to those who have violated our behavioral strictures is so stunted, and why our mainstream political discourses are so bereft of self-examination and searching social criticism. This historical resonance between the stigma of race and the stigma of imprisonment serves to keep alive in our public culture the subordinating social meanings that have always been associated with blackness. Race helps to explain why the United States is exceptional among the democratic industrial societies in the severity and extent of its punitive policy and in the paucity of its social-welfare institutions.

Slavery ended a long time ago, but the institution of chattel slavery and the ideology of racial subordination that accompanied it have cast a long shadow. I speak here of the history of lynching throughout the country; the racially biased policing and judging in the South under Jim Crow and in the cities of the Northeast, Midwest, and West to which blacks migrated after the First and Second World Wars; and the history of racial apartheid that ended only as a matter of law with the civil rights movement. It should come as no surprise that in the post–civil rights era, race, far from being peripheral, has been central to the evolution of American social policy.

The political scientist Vesla Mae Weaver, in a recently completed dissertation, examines policy history, public opinion, and media processes in an attempt to understand the role of race in this historic transformation of criminal justice. She argues—persuasively, I think—that the punitive turn represented a political response to the success of the civil rights movement. Weaver describes a process of "frontlash" in which opponents of the civil rights revolution sought to regain the upper hand by shifting to a new issue. Rather than reacting directly to civil rights developments, and thus continuing to fight a battle they had lost, those opponents—consider George Wallace's campaigns for the presidency, which drew so much support in states like Michigan and Wisconsin—shifted attention to a seemingly race-neutral concern over crime:

> Once the clutch of Jim Crow had loosened, opponents of civil rights shifted the "locus of attack" by injecting crime onto the agenda. Through the process of frontlash, rivals of civil rights progress defined racial discord as criminal and argued that crime legislation would be a panacea to racial unrest. This strategy both imbued crime with race and depoliticized racial struggle, a formula which foreclosed earlier "root causes" alternatives. Fusing anxiety

about crime to anxiety over racial change and riots, civil rights and racial disorder—initially defined as a problem of minority disenfranchisement—were defined as a crime problem, which helped shift debate from social reform to punishment.

Of course, this argument—for which Weaver adduces considerable circumstantial evidence—is speculative. But something interesting seems to have been going on in the late 1960s regarding the relationship between attitudes on race and social policy.

Before 1965, public attitudes on the welfare state and on race, as measured by the annually administered General Social Survey, varied from year to year independently of one another: you could not predict much about a person's attitudes on welfare politics by knowing his or her attitudes about race. After 1965, the attitudes moved in tandem, as welfare came to be seen as a race issue. The year-to-year correlation between an index measuring liberalism of racial attitudes and attitudes toward the welfare state over the interval 1950–1965 was 0.03. These same two series had a correlation of 0.68 over the period 1966–1996. The association in the American mind of race with welfare, and of race with crime, was achieved at a common historical moment. Crime-control institutions are part of a larger social-policy complex—they relate to and interact with the labor market, family-welfare efforts, and health and social-work activities. Indeed, Garland argues that the ideological approaches to welfare and crime control have marched rightward to a common beat: "The institutional and cultural changes that have occurred in the crime control field are analogous to those that have occurred in the welfare state more generally." Just as the welfare state came to be seen as a race issue, so, too, crime came to be seen as a race issue, and policies have been shaped by this perception.

Consider the tortured racial history of the War on Drugs. Blacks were twice as likely as whites to be arrested for a drug offense in 1975 but four times as likely by 1989. Throughout the 1990s, drug-arrest rates remained at historically unprecedented levels. Yet according to the National Survey on Drug Abuse, drug use among adults fell from 20 percent in 1979 to 11 percent in 2000. A similar trend occurred among adolescents. In the age groups 12–17 and 18–25, use of marijuana, cocaine, and heroin all peaked in the late 1970s and began a steady decline thereafter. Thus, a decline in drug use across the board had begun a decade before the draconian anti-drug efforts of the 1990s were initiated.

Of course, most drug arrests are for trafficking, not possession, so usage rates and arrest rates needn't be expected to be identical. Still, we do well to bear in mind that the social problem of illicit drug use is endemic to our whole society. Significantly, throughout the period

1979–2000, white high school seniors reported using drugs at a significantly higher rate than black high school seniors. High drug-usage rates in white, middle-class American communities in the early 1980s accounts for the urgency many citizens felt to mount a national attack on the problem. But how successful has the effort been, and at what cost?

Think of the cost this way: to save middle-class kids from the threat of a drug epidemic that might not have even existed by the time drug offense–fueled incarceration began its rapid increase in the 1980s, we criminalized underclass kids. Arrests went up, but drug prices have fallen sharply over the past 20 years—suggesting that the ratcheting up of enforcement has not made drugs harder to get on the street. The strategy clearly wasn't keeping drugs away from those who sought them. Not only are prices down, but the data show that drug-related visits to emergency rooms also rose steadily throughout the 1980s and 1990s.

An interesting case in point is New York City. Analyzing arrests by residential neighborhood and police precinct, the criminologist Jeffrey Fagan and his colleagues Valerie West and Jan Holland found that incarceration was highest in the city's poorest neighborhoods, though these were often not the neighborhoods in which crime rates were the highest. Moreover, they discovered a perverse effect of incarceration on crime: higher incarceration in a given neighborhood in one year seemed to predict higher crime rates in that same neighborhood one year later. This growth and persistence of incarceration over time, the authors concluded, was due primarily to the drug enforcement practices of police and to sentencing laws that require imprisonment for repeat felons. Police scrutiny was more intensive and less forgiving in high-incarceration neighborhoods, and parolees returning to such neighborhoods were more closely monitored. Thus, discretionary and spatially discriminatory police behavior led to a high and increasing rate of repeat prison admissions in the designated neighborhoods, even as crime rates fell.

Fagan, West, and Holland explain the effects of spatially concentrated urban anti-drug-law enforcement in the contemporary American metropolis. Buyers may come from any neighborhood and any social stratum. But the sellers—at least the ones who can be readily found hawking their wares on street corners and in public vestibules—come predominantly from the poorest, most non-white parts of the city. The police, with arrest quotas to meet, know precisely where to find them. The researchers conclude:

> Incarceration begets more incarceration, and incarceration also begets more crime, which in turn invites more aggressive enforcement, which then re-supplies incarceration . . . three

mechanisms . . . contribute to and reinforce incarceration in neighborhoods: the declining economic fortunes of former inmates and the effects on neighborhoods where they tend to reside, resource and relationship strains on families of prisoners that weaken the family's ability to supervise children, and voter disenfranchisement that weakens the political economy of neighborhoods.

The effects of imprisonment on life chances are profound. For incarcerated black men, hourly wages are 10 percent lower after prison than before. For all incarcerated men, the number of weeks worked per year falls by at least a third after their release.

So consider the nearly 60 percent of black male high school dropouts born in the late 1960s who are imprisoned before their fortieth year. While locked up, these felons are stigmatized—they are regarded as fit subjects for shaming. Their links to family are disrupted; their opportunities for work are diminished; their voting rights may be permanently revoked. They suffer civic excommunication. Our zeal for social discipline consigns these men to a permanent nether caste. And yet, since these men—whatever their shortcomings—have emotional and sexual and family needs, including the need to be fathers and lovers and husbands, we are creating a situation in which the children of this nether caste are likely to join a new generation of untouchables. This cycle will continue so long as incarceration is viewed as the primary path to social hygiene.

I HAVE BEEN EXPLORING THE ISSUE OF CAUSES: of why we took the punitive turn that has resulted in mass incarceration. But even if the racial argument about causes is inconclusive, the racial consequences are clear. To be sure, in the United States, as in any society, public order is maintained by the threat and use of force. We enjoy our good lives only because we are shielded by the forces of law and order, which keep the unruly at bay. Yet in this society, to a degree virtually unmatched in any other, those bearing the brunt of order enforcement belong in vastly disproportionate numbers to historically marginalized racial groups. Crime and punishment in America have a color.

In his fine 2006 study *Punishment and Inequality in America*, the Princeton University sociologist Bruce Western powerfully describes the scope, nature, and consequences of contemporary imprisonment. He finds that the extent of racial disparity in imprisonment rates is greater than in any other major arena of American social life: at eight to one, the black-white ratio of incarceration rates dwarfs the two-to-one ratio of unemployment rates, the three-to-one ratio of non-marital childbearing, the two-to-one ratio of infant-mortality rates and one-to-five ratio of net worth. While

3 out of 200 young whites were incarcerated in 2000, the rate for young blacks was 1 in 9. A black male resident of the state of California is more likely to go to a state prison than a state college.

The scandalous truth is that the police and penal apparatus are now the primary contact between adult black American men and the American state. Among black male high school dropouts aged twenty to forty, a third were locked up on any given day in 2000, fewer than 3 percent belonged to a union, and less than one-quarter were enrolled in any kind of social program. For these young men, government means, most saliently, coercion. Western estimates that nearly 60 percent of black male dropouts born between 1965 and 1969 were sent to prison on a felony conviction at least once before they reached the age of thirty-five.

One cannot reckon the world-historic American prison build-up over the past thirty-five years without calculating the enormous costs imposed upon the persons imprisoned, their families, and their communities. (Of course, this has not stopped many social scientists from pronouncing on the net benefits of incarceration without doing so.) Deciding on the weight to give to a "thug's" well-being—or to that of his wife or daughter or son—is a question of social morality, not social science. Nor can social science tell us how much additional cost borne by the offending class is justified in order to obtain a given increment of security or property or peace of mind for the rest of us. These are questions about the nature of the American state and its relationship to its people that transcend the categories of benefits and costs.

Yet the discourse surrounding punishment policy invariably discounts the humanity of the thieves, drug sellers, prostitutes, rapists, and, yes, those whom we put to death. It gives insufficient weight to the welfare, to the humanity, of those who are knitted together with offenders in webs of social and psychic affiliation. What is more, institutional arrangements for dealing with criminal offenders in the United States have evolved to serve expressive as well as instrumental ends. We have wanted to "send a message," and we have done so with a vengeance. In the process, we have created facts. We have answered the question, "Who is to blame for the domestic maladies that beset us?" We have constructed a national narrative. We have created scapegoats, indulged our need to feel virtuous, and assuaged our fears. We have met the enemy, and the enemy is them.

Incarceration keeps them away from us. Thus Garland writes, "The prison is used today as a kind of reservation, a quarantine zone in which purportedly dangerous individuals are segregated in the name of public safety." The boundary between prison and community is heavily patrolled and carefully monitored to prevent risks leaking out from one to the other. Those offenders who are released 'into the community' are subject to much tighter control than previously, and frequently find themselves returned to custody for failure to comply with the conditions that continue to restrict their freedom. For many of these parolees and ex-convicts, the 'community' into which they are released is actually a closely monitored terrain, a supervised space, lacking much of the liberty that one associates with 'normal life.'

Deciding how citizens of varied social rank within a common polity ought to relate to one another is a more fundamental consideration than deciding which crime-control policy is most efficient. The question of relationship, of solidarity, of who belongs to the body politic and who deserves exclusion—these are philosophical concerns of the highest order. A decent society will on occasion resist the efficient course of action, for the simple reason that to follow it would be to act as though we were not the people we have determined ourselves to be: a people conceived in liberty and dedicated to the proposition that we all are created equal. Assessing the propriety of creating a racially defined pariah class in the middle of our great cities at the start of the twenty-first century presents us with just such a case.

My recitation of the brutal facts about punishment in today's America may sound to some like a primal scream at this monstrous social machine that is grinding poor black communities to dust. And I confess that these brutal facts do at times leave me inclined to cry out in despair. But my argument is analytical, not existential. Its principal thesis is this: we law-abiding, middle-class Americans have made decisions about social policy and incarceration, and we benefit from those decisions, and that means from a system of suffering, rooted in state violence, meted out at our request. We had choices and we decided to be more punitive. Our society—the society we have made—creates criminogenic conditions in our sprawling urban ghettos, and then acts out rituals of punishment against them as some awful form of human sacrifice.

This situation raises a moral problem that we cannot avoid. We cannot pretend that there are more important problems in our society, or that this circumstance is the necessary solution to other, more pressing problems—unless we are also prepared to say that we have turned our backs on the ideal of equality for all citizens and abandoned the principles of justice. We ought to ask ourselves two questions: Just what manner of people are we Americans? And in light of this, what are our obligations to our fellow citizens—even those who break our laws?

TO ADDRESS THESE QUESTIONS, WE NEED to think about the evaluation of our prison system as a problem in the theory of distributive justice—not the purely procedural idea of ensuring equal treatment before the law and thereafter letting the chips fall where they may, but the rather more demanding ideal of substantive racial justice. The goal is to bring about, through conventional social policy and far-reaching institutional reforms, a situation in which the history of racial oppression is no longer so evident in the disparate life experiences of those who descend from slaves.

And I suggest we approach that problem from the perspective of John Rawls's theory of justice. First, we should think about justice from an "original position" behind a "veil of ignorance" that obstructs from view our own situation, including our class, race, gender, and talents. We need to ask what rules we would pick if we seriously imagined that we could turn out to be anyone in the society. Second, following Rawls's "difference principle," we should permit inequalities only if they work to improve the circumstances of the least advantaged members of society. But here, the object of moral inquiry is not the distribution among individuals of wealth and income, but instead the distribution of a negative good, punishment, among individuals and, importantly, racial groups.

So put yourself in John Rawls's original position and imagine that you could occupy any rank in the social hierarchy. Let me be more concrete: imagine that you could be born a black American male outcast shuffling between prison and the labor market on his way to an early death to the chorus of "nigger" or "criminal" or "dummy." Suppose we had to stop thinking of us and them. What social rules would we pick if we actually thought that they could be us? I expect that we would still pick some set of punishment institutions to contain bad behavior and protect society. But wouldn't we pick arrangements that respected the humanity of each

RACE, INCARCERATION,
        AND AMERICAN VALUES

individual and of those they are connected to through bonds of social and psychic affiliation? If any one of us had a real chance of being one of those faces looking up from the bottom of the well—of being the least among us—then how would we talk publicly about those who break our laws? What would we do with juveniles who go awry, who roam the streets with guns and sometimes commit acts of violence? What weight would we give to various elements in the deterrence-retribution-incapacitation-rehabilitation calculus, if we thought that calculus could end up being applied to our own children, or to us? How would we apportion blame and affix responsibility for the cultural and social pathologies evident in some quarters of our society if we envisioned that we ourselves might well have been born into the social margins where such pathology flourishes?

If we were to take these questions as seriously as we should, then we would, I expect, reject a pure ethic of personal responsibility as the basis for distributing punishment. Issues about responsibility are complex, and involve a kind of division of labor—what Rawls called a "social division of responsibility" between "citizens as a collective body" and individuals: when we hold a person responsible for his or her conduct—by establishing laws, investing in their enforcement, and consigning some persons to prisons—we need also to think about whether we have done our share in ensuring that each person faces a decent set of opportunities for a good life. We need to ask whether we as a society have fulfilled our collective responsibility to ensure fair conditions for each person—for each life that might turn out to be our life.

We would, in short, recognize a kind of social responsibility, even for the wrongful acts freely chosen by individual persons. I am not arguing that people commit crimes because they have no choices, and that in this sense the "root causes" of crime are social; individuals always have choices. My point is that responsibility is a matter of ethics, not social science. Society at large is implicated in an individual person's choices because we have acquiesced in—perhaps actively supported, through our taxes and votes, words and deeds—social arrangements that work to our benefit and his detriment, and which shape his consciousness and sense of identity in such a way that the choices he makes, which we may condemn, are nevertheless compelling to him—an entirely understandable response to circumstance. Closed and bounded social structures—like racially homogeneous urban ghettos—create contexts where "pathological" and "dysfunctional" cultural forms emerge, but these forms are neither intrinsic to the people caught in these structures nor independent of the behavior of people who stand outside them.

Thus, a central reality of our time is the fact that there has opened a wide racial gap in the acquisition of cognitive skills, the extent of law-abidingness, the stability of family relations, the attachment to the work force, and the like. This disparity in human development is, as a historical matter, rooted in political, economic, social, and cultural factors peculiar to this society and reflective of its unlovely racial history: it is a societal, not communal or personal, achievement. At the level of the individual case we must, of course, act as if this were not so. There could be no law, no civilization, without the imputation to particular persons of responsibility for their wrongful acts. But the sum of a million cases, each one rightly judged on its merits to be individually fair, may nevertheless constitute a great historic wrong. The state does not only deal with individual cases. It also makes policies in the aggregate, and the consequences of these policies are more or less knowable. And who can honestly say—who can look in the mirror and say with a straight face—that we now have laws and policies that we would endorse if we did not know our own situation and genuinely considered the possibility that we might be the least advantaged?

Even if the current racial disparity in punishment in our country gave evidence of no overt racial discrimination—and, perhaps needless to say, I view that as a wildly optimistic supposition—it would still be true that powerful forces are at work to perpetuate the consequences of a universally acknowledged wrongful past. This is in the first instance a matter of interpretation—of the narrative overlay that we impose upon the facts.

The tacit association in the American public's imagination of "blackness" with "unworthiness" or "dangerousness" has obscured a fundamental ethical point about responsibility, both collective and individual, and promoted essentialist causal misattributions: when confronted by the facts of racially disparate achievement, racially disproportionate crime rates, and racially unequal school achievement, observers will have difficulty identifying with the plight of a group of people whom they (mistakenly) think are simply "reaping what they have sown." Thus, the enormous racial disparity in the imposition of social exclusion, civic ex-communication, and lifelong disgrace has come to seem legitimate, even necessary: we fail to see how our failures as a collective body are implicated in this disparity. We shift all the responsibility onto their shoulders, only by irresponsibly—indeed, immorally—denying our own. And yet, this entire dynamic has its roots in past unjust acts that were perpetrated on the basis of race.

Given our history, producing a racially defined nether caste through the ostensibly neutral application of law should be profoundly offensive to our ethical sensibilities—to the principles we proudly assert as our own. Mass incarceration has now become a principal vehicle for the reproduction of racial hierarchy in our society. Our country's policymakers need to do something about it. And all of us are ultimately responsible for making sure that they do.

II

Forum

Pamela S. Karlan

LOURY HAS COMPARED AMERICA TODAY
TO its own past: the dishonor and dehumanization of incarceration to the dishonor
and dehumanization of slavery. He has also
compared it to other nations' present, in a
world where America imprisons a quarter
of the people now in prison. As Loury suggests, voter disenfranchisement plays a large
role in this story.

The Fifteenth Amendment to the U.S. Constitution, ratified in 1870, prohibits denial or abridgement of the right to vote because of race, color, or previous condition of servitude. According to the 1870 census, there were then approximately 1,083,484 black men in the United States over the age of twenty. Since every state then had a voting age of twenty-one and no state then allowed women to vote, we can conclude that, at most, the Fifteenth Amendment enfranchised 1,083,484 African-Americans.

By contrast, in the 1996 presidential election, 1.4 million black men were *dis*enfranchised by the United States' draconian laws, many for crimes so minor that even with our savage incarceration policies, they were never sentenced to even a day in jail. In the winter of 1988, for example, Sanford McLaughlin tendered a check for $150 to the Local Jitney Jungle, for which he had, in the terms lawyers use, insufficient funds on deposit. In other words, he bounced a check. He was convicted of a misdemeanor count of obtaining money under false pretenses, fined $75 plus costs, ordered to pay $150 restitution, and placed on six months' non-reporting probation. Under Article XI, § 241 of the Mississippi Constitution of 1890, he was disenfranchised—for life.

An international comparison is also illuminating. At one time, all felonies imposed a civil death on convicted persons, denying them many of the standard rights of citizenship. But that has not been federal law, in the United States or elsewhere, for centuries. Prisoners—let alone offenders who have served their sentences or who receive punishments other than imprisonment—vote in countries as diverse as the Czech Republic, Denmark, France, Israel, Japan, Kenya, the Netherlands, and Zimbabwe. Israel sets up polling places in prisons and detention centers, and its laws even permitted the man who assassinated Yitzhak Rabin to vote for his successor. The Supreme Courts of Canada and South Africa both issued opinions in the last few years requiring those nations to permit incarcerated citizens to vote. Consider a statement from the opinion of South African Justice Albie Sachs, a man who spent time in jail during the apartheid era:

> The vote of each and every citizen is a badge of dignity and of personhood. Quite literally, it says that everybody counts. In a country of great disparities of wealth and power it declares that whoever we are, whether rich or poor, exalted or disgraced, we all belong to the same democratic South African nation; that our destinies are intertwined in a single interactive polity.

Scholars do not entirely agree on when offender disenfranchisement laws began to appear in the United States. A law student writing thirty years ago cited a provision in the Virginia constitution in 1776 as the first such law. More recent work by sociologists Chris Uggen and Jeff Manza identifies the first provision as appearing sometime in the 1810s. As late as the 1850s, however, a majority of states had no felon disenfranchisement. But by the end of the 1860s—the decade of emancipation—two-thirds of the states had enacted disenfranchisement provisions. And the link to race was quite explicit. Consider the Alabama constitutional convention of 1901. Section 182 of that constitution disenfranchised individuals convicted of "any crime . . . involving moral turpitude." John B. Knox, president of the convention, stated the purpose of this provision in his opening address: "And what is it that we want to do? Why it is within the limits imposed by the Federal Constitution, to establish white supremacy in this State." The list of misdemeanors that would trigger disenfranchisement included such crimes as vagrancy and living in adultery, thought to be more commonly committed by blacks.

In 1985, the Supreme Court, in a unanimous opinion by Justice William Rehnquist, voted to strike down section 182. The basis for the Court's ruling was that this offender disenfranchisement was tainted by a racist purpose. But the same Justice Rehnquist who could see the racism in Alabama's constitution was also the author of another Supreme Court decision, in *Richardson v. Ramirez* (1974), upholding the general permissibility of offender disenfranchisement. Justice Rehnquist read the second section of the Fourteenth Amendment as a green light for such disenfranchisement. That provision was designed—every historian agrees—to *protect* black voting rights. It threatened southern states with the loss of their seats in Congress and their votes in the Electoral College, if they continued to bar blacks from voting:

But when the right to vote at any election . . . is denied to any of the male inhabitants of such State, being twenty-one years of age, and citizens of the United States, or in any way abridged, except for participation in rebellion, or other crime, the basis of representation therein shall be reduced in the proportion which the number of such male citizens shall bear to the whole number of male citizens twenty-one years of age in such State.

The Court read that provision's failure to penalize states that abridged the right to vote "for participation in . . . other crime" as an affirmative license to do so. The results are devastating.

The actual impact of felon disenfranchisement today is greater than at any point in our history. The United States incarcerates proportionally more than six times as many individuals as it did when *Richardson* was litigated. Current laws disenfranchise approximately 3.9 million voting-age citizens. More than one-third have completed their sentences. When we add those on probation or parole, nearly three-quarters of disenfranchised citizens are not in prison.

Felon disenfranchisement has decimated the potential black electorate. The problem is especially striking in states with lifetime disqualification laws. In Alabama and Florida, nearly a third of all black men are permanently disenfranchised. In Iowa, Mississippi, Virginia, and Wyoming, roughly a quarter are permanently barred.

The potential effects of this massive exclusion were driven home by the agonizingly close 2000 presidential race in Florida in which George Bush ostensibly won the state by 530-something votes. Florida disenfranchises more people than any other state—approximately 827,000. Slightly over 600,000 of those individuals have completed their sentences and have been discharged entirely from the criminal justice system. Approximately 10.5 percent of the state's adult black population was disenfranchised compared with 4.4 percent of the non-black population. A recent study by Chris Uggen and Jeff Manza estimated that, had ex-offenders who had completed their sentences been permitted to vote—presumably at the same rate as their socioeconomically comparable, but not disenfranchised, peers—Al Gore would have carried Florida by more than 31,000 votes.

But one need not indulge in counterfactual hypotheticals to see how felon disenfranchisement laws distorted the 2000 election. Florida's law did not only exclude hundreds of thousands of ex-offenders from the polls. As the U.S. Commission on Civil Rights found, the state disenfranchised significant numbers of eligible voters as well, due to a profoundly flawed purge process. For example, individuals were removed from the voting rolls because their names resembled those of convicted felons. Statewide, the purge removed 8,456 black voters from the rolls; after the election, of the 4,847 people who appealed, 2,430 were restored to the list as eligible voters. In one large county, the supervisor of elections later estimated that 15 percent of the people purged were in fact eligible to vote, and a majority of those purged were African-American. In short, Florida showed the "collateral damage" that criminal disenfranchisement can cause—denying indisputably qualified citizens and wholly blameless communities the ability to elect the candidate of their choice.

There is another racially salient political consequence of disenfranchisement. Under the "usual residence rule," the Census Bureau counts incarcerated individuals as residents of the jurisdiction in which they are incarcerated. In many states, this results in largely white, rural communities benefiting from increased population totals at the expense of the heavily urban, overwhelmingly minority communities from which most inmates come. Peter Wagner, who runs an organization called Prisoners of the Census, reports that although rural counties contain only 20 percent of the U.S. population, 60 percent of new prison construction occurs there.

Because state legislative districts are also based on population, prisoners serve as inert ballast in the redistricting process. For example, in New York, seven conservative upstate Republicans represent state senatorial districts that comply with one-person, one-vote only because prisoners are included in the population base. But these officials are neither descriptively nor substantively "representative" of their inmate "constituents." For example, one of the upstate districts is represented by Republican state senator Dale Volker. There are more than 11,000 inmates at eight state correctional facilities in his district. Given the economic benefits prisons provide to otherwise hard-hit rural communities, it is hardly surprising that Senator Volker is a leading defender of New York's draconian drug laws, which have resulted in a huge prison population. A number of commentators have compared this "usual residence rule" to the notorious "three-fifths" clause in the original Constitution, which enhanced the political clout of slave-holding states by including slaves in the population base for calculating Congressional seats and electoral votes.

The entire political effect of criminal disenfranchisement laws is impossible to calculate. But it is telling that the states that disenfranchise the largest number of citizens also have some of the most draconian criminal codes, and it is not entirely clear in which direction the causal arrows run. It may well be that it is precisely because their electorates are skewed that they enact increasingly harsh laws that reinforce the skew. This may be especially true to the extent that the criminal law is enforced in a racially biased or disproportionate way. Angela Behrens's recent work argues that perceived "racial threat" is a major variable in predicting a state's disenfranchisement practices. She concludes:

> The racial composition of state prisons is firmly associated with the adoption of state felon disenfranchisement laws. States with greater nonwhite prison populations have been more likely to ban convicted felons from voting than states with proportionally fewer nonwhites in the criminal justice system.

Conversely, states with a small proportion of African-American prisoners are most likely to abolish ex-felon voting restrictions.

Despite this discouraging reality, the tenor of the debate over felon disenfranchisement has taken a remarkable turn. After a generation of unsuccessful litigation against disenfranchisement laws, *politics* has made some dramatic strides. Recent public opinion surveys find that over 80 percent of Americans believe that ex-offenders should regain their right to vote at some point, and more than 40 percent would allow offenders on probation or parole to vote. A conservative Republican governor of Alabama signed legislation making it easier for ex-offenders to regain their voting rights. Several other states have made the restoration of voting rights automatic upon completion of an offender's sentence or within a short period of time thereafter.

For those of us who can vote, the least we can do is give our votes only to candidates who promise to restore the voting rights of former offenders.

Loïc Wacquant

As bad as the story Loury tells us is, the reality on the ground is much worse. The penal state is larger, meaner, more entrenched, and more intrusive. And it has a more concentrated and pernicious impact on lower-class African-Americans trapped in the vestiges of the dark ghetto.

The brute increase in the population behind bars—from 380,000 in 1975 to over 2 million by 2000—is only part of the story of the expansion of the penal state. This increase is remarkable for having been fueled not by the lengthening of the average sentence as in previous eras, but primarily by the surge in prison admissions (which ballooned from 159,000 in 1980 to 665,000 in 1997). But the "vertical" rise of the penal system has been exceeded by its "horizontal" spread: the ranks of those kept in the shadow of the prison via probation (four million) and parole (about one million) have swelled even more than the population under lock. The reach of penal authorities has also been enlarged by the exponential growth in the size, scope, and uses of criminal justice databases, which contained some 60 million files in 2000. The advent of penal "Big Government" was made possible by stupendous increases in funding (prison and jail expenditures in America jumped from $7 billion in 1980 to $57 billion in 2000) and the infusion of one million staff, which has made corrections the third largest employer in the nation, behind Manpower and Wal-Mart.

Like other analysts of the U.S. penal scene, Loury calls this unprecedented expansion *mass* incarceration. This is a mischaracterization. *Mass* incarceration suggests that confinement concerns large swaths of the citizenry (as with the mass media, mass culture, mass unemployment, etc.). But the expansion and intensification of the activities of the police, courts, and prison over the past quarter-century have been finely targeted by class, ethnicity, and place, leading to what is better referred to as the *hyper*-incarceration of one particular category: lower-class black men in the crumbling ghetto. The rest of society—including middle-class blacks—is practically untouched. Indeed, had the penal state been rolled out indiscriminately through policies resulting in the capture of vast a number of whites and middle-class citizens, its growth would have been derailed quickly by political action.

The welcome focus on race, crime, and punishment that has dominated discussions of the prison boom has also hidden from view the fact that inmates are first and foremost *poor people*. Consider the social profile of the clientele of the nation's jails: fewer than half of inmates held a full-time job at the time of their arraignment and two-thirds issue from households with annual income amounting to less than *half* of the so-called poverty line.

Race comes second. The ethno-racial makeup of convicts has flip-flopped completely in four decades, turning over from 70 percent white and 30 percent "other" at the close of World War II to 70 percent black and Latino and 30 percent white by century's close. This inversion, which took off after the mid-1970s, is all the more stunning when one considers that the criminal population has become *whiter* during that period: The share of African-Americans among individuals arrested by the police for the four most serious violent offenses (murder, rape, robbery, aggravated assault) dropped from 51 percent in 1973 to 43 percent in 1996. The rapid "blackening" of the prison population, even as crime "whitened," is due exclusively to the increase in the incarceration rates of *lower-class* blacks. In his book *Punishment and Inequality in America*, Bruce Western produces a stunning statistic: whereas the cumulative risk of imprisonment for African-American males without a high school education tripled between 1978 and 1998 to reach the astonishing rate of 59 percent, the chance that black men with some college education would serve time at any point in their lives *decreased* from 6 percent to 5 percent over the same period.

How is it possible that criminal laws ostensibly written to avoid class and color bias would lead to throwing so many (sub)proletarian black men under lock, and not other black men? The class gradient in racialized imprisonment was obtained by targeting one particular place: the remnants of the black ghetto. I insist here on the word remnants, because the ghetto of old, which held in its grip a unified if stratified black community, is no more. The communal Black Belt of the Fordist era, described by a long lineage of distinguished black sociologists, from W.E.B. Du Bois to E. Franklin Frazier to St. Clair Drake and Horace Cayton to Kenneth Clark, imploded in the 1960s, to be replaced by a dual structure: a degraded *hyperghetto*, doubly segregated by race and class, and the *satellite black middle-class districts* that mushroomed in adjacent areas after the mass exodus of whites to the suburbs.

There is a tight causal linkage between hyper-ghettoization and hyper-incarceration, but to see it we must break out of the narrow ambit of the "crime and punishment" paradigm. A simple ratio suffices to demonstrate that crime cannot be the cause behind carceral growth: the number of clients of state and federal prisons boomed from 21 convicts per 10,000 "index crimes" in 1975 to 106 per 10,000 in 1999. In other words, keeping the crime rate constant shows that the American penal state is five times more punitive today than it was three decades ago.

We also need to recognize that the ghetto is an instrument of ethno-racial control in the city. Like the Jewish ghetto in Renaissance Europe, the Black Belt of the American metropolis in the Fordist age combined four elements—stigma, constraint, spatial confinement, and institutional encasement—to permit the economic exploitation and social ostracization of a population deemed congenitally inferior. Succeeding slavery and Jim Crow, the ghetto was the third "peculiar institution" entrusted with defining, confining, and controlling African-Americans in the urban industrial order.

Penal expansion after the mid-1970s is a political response to the collapse of the ghetto. But why did the ghetto collapse? One cause is the postindustrial economic transition that shifted employment from manufacturing to services, from central city to suburb, and from the rustbelt to the sunbelt and low-wage foreign countries. Together with renewed immigration, this shift made black workers redundant and undercut the role of the ghetto as a reservoir of unskilled labor.

The second cause is the political displacement provoked by the Great White Migration to the suburbs. From the 1950s to the 1970s, millions of white families fled the metropolis in response to the influx of African-Americans from the rural south. This demographic upheaval, subsidized by the federal government, weakened cities in the national electoral system and reduced the political pull of African-Americans.

The third force behind the breakdown of the ghetto as ethno-racial container is black protest, culminating with the civil rights legislation, the budding of Black Power activism and the explosion of riots that rocked the country between 1964 and 1968.

Unlike Jim Crow, then, the ghetto was not dismantled by forceful government action. It was left to crumble onto itself, trapping lower-class African-Americans in a vortex of unemployment, poverty, and crime, abetted by the joint withdrawal of the wage-labor market and the welfare state, while the growing black middle class achieved limited social and spatial separation. As the ghetto lost its economic function and proved unable to ensure ethno-racial closure, the prison was called upon to help contain a population widely viewed as deviant, destitute, and dangerous. In so doing it returned to its original historical mission: not to stem crime, but to manage dispossessed and dishonored populations marginalized by economic transformation.

I want to warn here against the ahistorical invocation of the historical legacy of slavery: the monstrous penal state that now clutches the black subproletariat is not "neoslavery" and penitentiaries are not latter-day plantations (if only because inmates produce no economic value and constitute a colossal fiscal drain on the nation). Its rise is not a delayed resurgence or an updated version of bondage or Jim Crow. This is a story not from 400 years ago, but from 50 years ago: the new institutional contraption formed by the deteriorating hyperghetto and the hypertrophied prison is a response to the crash of the ghetto as a distinctive apparatus of ethnoracial control.

We must also avoid the artificial analytical freezing of race: the denegated ethnic division we label "race" is not a timeless constant. Even as the rigid black-white cleavage has been perpetuated, the constellation of properties believed to characterize blacks and justify their ostracization in national life has changed. Bluntly put in terms of vituperative stereotypes, Sambo is not Steppin' Fetchit is not Willie Horton. In the post-Keynesian era of deregulated labor and hyperincarceration, it is no longer unworthiness but *dangerousness* that stamps the hegemonic "biased cognition" about blacks, precisely because the prison has become the primary machine for signifying and enforcing a class-graduated conception of race in the country.

Yet the tightening nexus between the hyperghetto and the prison does not tell the whole story of race and the penal institution in post-Fordist America. The unleashing of a voracious prison apparatus after the mid-1970s partakes of a broader restructuring of the state, tending to criminalize poverty and its consequences so as to impose insecure jobs as the normal horizon of work for the unskilled factions of the postindustrial proletariat. The sudden hypertrophy of the penal state was thus complemented by the planned atrophy of the social state, culminating with the 1996 law on "Personal Responsibility and Work Opportunity," which replaced the right to "welfare" with the obligation of "workfare." Together, workfare and prisonfare ensnare the marginal populations of the metropolis in a *carceral-assistential net* designed to steer them toward deregulated employment through moral retraining and material suasion and, if they prove too recalcitrant, to warehouse them in the devastated core of the urban Black Belt and in the penitentiaries that have become its direct satellites.

This dynamic coupling of social and penal policy operates through a familiar division of labor between the sexes: the public aid bureaucracy, reconverted into an administrative springboard to subpoverty employment, takes up the task of inculcating the duty of working for work's sake to poor women (and indirectly to their children), while the penal quartet formed by the police, the court, the prison, and the probation or parole officer shoulders the mission of taming their men. This means that we cannot hope to untie the knot of race and imprisonment if we do not link hyperin-carceration and workfare.

If my diagnosis is correct, then moral exhortation about race and incarceration on grounds of civic inclusiveness will not get us very far. It is precisely because "we" are *not* "in this together," as Loury proffers, that America's punitive penal state was allowed to grow to outlandish proportions, in linked relation to the implosion of the dark ghetto and to the shift from welfare to workfare. And, for this very reason, penal containment is unlikely to mobilize large segments of the citizenry. Moreover, the American electorate has so far extended constant support for the far-reaching retooling of the state of which hyperincarceration is but one component.

Instead of rhetorical appeals to common moral values, I would give priority to political strategies aimed at stressing common interests and the shared burdens of further carceral escalation. Such a strategy would highlight the extravagant financial costs of continued hyperincarceration; trace the manifold ways in which it destabilizes lower-class families and neighborhoods, aggravating the very social ills it is supposed to remedy; and revise as well as revive alternative strategies that prioritize social and medical treatments over penal ones.

The rise of a hypertrophic and hyperactive penal state that practices carceral affirmative action through a class filter is not a moral dilemma, as Gunnar Myrdal famously argued in 1944, but a political problem. Here I must side with Kenneth Clark when, writing amidst the wave of black revolts that shook up the American metropolis in the 1960s, he diagnosed the predicament of the dark ghetto as a question of power and its distribution. Half a century later, this remains true of the fiendish institutional contraption that now links workfare and prisonfare, on the one side, and prisons and the hyperghetto, on the other.

Tommie Shelby

GLENN LOURY RAISES THREE DISTINCT questions of justice. The first is: do the punishments meted out frequently fail to fit the crimes committed by the black urban poor? Given the long sentences for nonviolent offenders, stiff penalties for minor parole violations, and disfranchisement of ex-convicts who have completed their sentences, his answer is yes. The criminal justice system and U.S. society more broadly have become excessively punitive. This suggests the need for reform of the penal code to ensure that it is fair, effective, and humane.

A second question is whether mass incarceration has had a disproportionate impact on African-Americans. Loury answers yes, and suggests that this fact, in itself, should lead us to reconsider our current punishment practices. Given our long history of racial injustice, he argues, we cannot tolerate a criminal justice system that creates a stigmatized racial caste.

The third question is: are these excessive penalties for nonviolent crime imposed because their consequences fall largely on a stigmatized group whom most care little about? Here his answer is also affirmative. However, he does not want to put too much weight on this claim, arguing instead that the fact that the penalties have a disproportionate impact on African-

Americans is reason enough to call for change. This strategy, as I shall explain, is a mistake.

All three questions fall under what John Rawls calls "nonideal theory." If ideal theory investigates the principles a fully just society should embody, nonideal theory studies how we should respond to *injustice*. One dimension of this theory involves responding to an individual's failure to comply with the requirements of just institutions (e.g., obeying the law). The other dimension concerns how to rectify injustices in a society's basic institutional arrangement. So there is the degree of *individual compliance*, measured by the extent to which persons follow the rules and regulations laid down by society, and there is the degree of *collective compliance*, measured by the extent to which the main institutions of social life are just.

Thus, nonideal theory is relevant to Loury's discussion of the U.S. criminal justice system in at least two distinct ways. He could try to figure out how a just society should respond to individual noncompliance—the failure of individuals to obey the law—when the offender is from a historically oppressed racial group still burdened by socioeconomic disadvantages. Or he could attempt to determine the progressive response to the criminal behavior of the worst off in an unjust society in need of fundamental reform, a society with a high degree of collective noncompliance.

The extent to which Loury is concerned with a just system of *punishment* as opposed to the justice of the overall *sociopolitical order* of which the penal system is one element is not entirely clear. All three questions could be approached with a view to penal reform or with a view to substantial structural change in our society or, of course, with a view to both. He sometimes suggests that his sole concern is with penal sanctions, raising larger issues only insofar as they bear on criminal justice. For instance, when he invokes Rawls's theory of justice and the conceptual framework of the original position with its famous veil of ignorance, he asks: what principles of *punishment* would we choose if we thought that we could be the criminals in the dark ghetto to which these principles would apply? That is a good question. But it does not get at the basic issues of justice that Rawls sought to address.

Loury also invokes Rawls's difference principle, which holds that the only socioeconomic inequalities that are morally justified are ones that work to the advantage of the worst off. It could not be more clear that the vast inequalities in income and wealth in the United States today do not redound to the benefit of the worst off—that is, those without marketable talents. Yet Loury does not draw out the implications of this principle in thinking about the black urban poor's legitimate claims for redress, except to assert that, given our history of racial injustice, we should not be indifferent to contemporary racial inequality.

Do not misunderstand me. Penal reform is an urgent problem that demands immediate practical responses aimed at amelioration, not necessarily at full social justice. It would be irresponsible and heartless to ignore present suffering because we regard penal reform as too modest to get at the underlying unfairness in our social system. Yet we should also attend to these fundamental structural injustices. The fight for equal citizenship for all African-Americans has already been a long one, and though many are tired of carrying it on, it is yet to be won. But the current struggle is not, at its core, about mass incarceration.

Loury's critique of the conservative ideology of personal responsibility strikes me as a good place to enter the debate over what equal citizenship requires. There is a failure in the public discourse and even in much social-scientific discourse to appreciate the complex interaction between individual choices and social structure. Because of the stigma attached to blackness, the social consequences of this interaction are too often attributed solely to individual values and character. Yet individuals are forced to make choices in an environment they did not choose. They would surely prefer to have a broader array of good opportunities. The question we should be asking—not instead of but in addition to questions about penal policy—is whether the denizens of the ghetto are entitled to a better set of options, and if so, whose responsibility it is to provide them.

Moreover, as Loury argues, too many affluent citizens do not view these disadvantaged persons as fellow citizens. Rather, they see them as a lazy, irresponsible, and dangerous out-group that must be contained. I suspect that the affluent may also be led to this view because they refuse to be honest with themselves about two realities: that the society in which they live is profoundly unjust, and that the privileged positions they themselves occupy have been obtained by exploiting a manifestly unfair opportunity structure.

It is a truism about human nature—one emphasized by Max Weber—that the privileged want to believe that they merit their advantages and that the disadvantaged deserve all their hardships. In view of this human impulse, progressives must continuously emphasize that the ghetto poor have not received their due, not just in terms of the criminal justice system, but in terms of the full complement of rights, services, and opportunities to which they are entitled as equal citizens.

Loury recognizes the injustices that have led to mass incarceration. Indeed, his analysis provides the basis for a more fundamental critique of U.S. society. For instance, his argument about racial stigma suggests that there is discrimination not only in informal contexts but in the operation of our most important institutions. Given the power of racial stigma to affect our judgment and behavior, such personal racism must surely spill over into the administration of basic social institutions, not just into the criminal justice system but into the schools, the labor market, electoral processes, social services, and the housing market. This constitutes institutional racism. So why not call for more rigorous antidiscrimination laws and greater investment in their enforcement?

Loury also emphasizes the contemporary relevance of slavery and Jim Crow. He recognizes that many blacks have inherited disadvantages as a legacy of racial injustice. He urges us to be mindful of this shameful history when we make crime policy. But he stops short of demanding compensatory measures such as, say, investing heavily in the development of human capital in poor communities or helping poor people to buy homes in mixed-income neighborhoods. Moreover, citizens cannot have equal life chances when the quality of education varies so dramatically among neighborhoods that are segregated by race and class.

Given the myriad injustices that the ghetto poor face, why should racial *parity* be the goal? If there were the same percentage of whites as there are now blacks in prison, in poverty, faced with only low-paying jobs, forced to attend substandard schools, and without adequate health care, should we think that social justice had been achieved? Such parity is what you strive for when you think that full social justice is not feasible or worth fighting for—or when you have no real investment in bringing about a just society.

Now, the political environment may be so inhospitable to progressive change that racial parity may be as much as can realistically be accomplished in the immediate future. Moreover, attempting to achieve such parity might be a useful intermediate goal, perhaps a way to weaken the association of blackness with crime and moral vice. But it is important to make clear—particularly to those languishing in the ghettos of the United States—that this is pure pragmatism, or better, that this is the next practical step in a long-range struggle for a truly just society. Otherwise, the self-respect of the ghetto poor will be threatened, and they would be right to be suspicious of the motives of affluent would-be benefactors and allies, given their obvious stake in holding on to their privileges.

The point here is actually rather old. It comes from W.E.B. Du Bois's critique of Booker T. Washington at the turn of the twentieth century. Washington downplayed the importance of civil rights and social equality for the newly freed persons, suggesting that they were not ready for such civic responsibilities and that racial integration was too much to ask. He also urged Southern blacks to reconcile with their white oppressors without demanding compensation for past wrongs. He took this accommodationist stance—for which he is famous or infamous, depending on one's point of view—because he thought this was the best way to help his people in racist America. Du Bois, too, recognized that full social justice for black people was not on the horizon. Nevertheless he insisted on making clear that blacks knew what their rights were, that they knew they were being unjustly denied equal citizenship, and that they would not rest until they had *all* the liberties and opportunities due them as equal members of the republic. This is the only dignified way to live under unjust conditions.

So I urge us to make a clean break with Washington's political outlook on race, by openly demanding full justice for all citizens, and attacking racism and socioeconomic inequality directly. As Du Bois often emphasized, we should not sacrifice principle for expediency and we should keep our just grievances before the public, even as we fight against formidable odds and even as we try to save as many of the most vulnerable and neglected as possible.

ABOUT THE CONTRIBUTORS

GLENN C. LOURY is Merton P. Stoltz Professor of the Social Sciences in the department of economics at Brown University. A 2002 Carnegie Scholar, he is author of *The Anatomy of Racial Inequality*.

PAMELA S. KARLAN is Kenneth and Harle Montgomery Professor of Public Interest Law at Stanford University. Prior to entering teaching, she served as assistant counsel at the NAACP Legal Defense and Educational Fund, where she specialized in voting rights cases. Professor Karlan continues to litigate voting rights cases before the United States Supreme Court and other federal courts. She is co-author of the leading casebook on regulation of voting rights.

TOMMIE SHELBY is Professor of African and African-American Studies and of Philosophy at Harvard University. He is author of *We Who Are Dark: The Philosophical Foundations of Black Solidarity* and co-editor (with Derrick Darby) of *Hip Hop and Philosophy: Rhyme 2 Reason*. He is coeditor of *Transition* magazine.

LOÏC WACQUANT is Professor of Sociology at the University of California, Berkeley and Researcher at the Centre de sociologie européenne, Paris. His works have appeared in a dozen languages. His recent books include *Urban Outcasts: A Comparative Sociology of Advanced Marginality* and the forthcoming *Punishing the Poor: The New Government of Social Insecurity*.

BOSTON REVIEW BOOKS

Boston Review Books are accessible, short books that take ideas seriously. They are animated by hope, committed to equality, and convinced that the imagination eludes political categories. The editors aim to establish a public space in which people can loosen the hold of conventional preconceptions and start to reason together across the lines others are so busily drawing.